D1543075

JBIOG
Jones
Zack, Bill

Chipper Jones

BASEBALL LEGENDS

CHELSEA HOUSE PUBLISHERS

BASEBALL LEGENDS

CHIPPER JONES

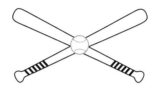

Bill Zack

Introduction by
Jim Murray

Senior Consultant
Earl Weaver

CHELSEA HOUSE PUBLISHERS
Philadelphia

Produced by Choptank Syndicate, Inc.

Editor and Picture Researcher: Norman L. Macht
Production Coordinator and Editorial Assistant: Mary E. Hull
Design and Production: Lisa Hochstein

CHELSEA HOUSE PUBLISHERS

Editor in Chief: Stephen Reginald
Managing Editor: James Gallagher
Production Manager: Pamela Loos
Art Director: Sara Davis
Director of Photography: Judy L. Hasday
Senior Production Editor: Lisa Chippendale
Publishing Coordinator: James McAvoy
Cover Design and Digital Illustration: Keith Trego

Cover Photos: AP/Wide World Photos

The Chelsea House World Wide Web site
address is http://www.chelseahouse.com

3 5 7 9 8 6 4 2

Library of Congress Cataloging-in-Publication Data

Zack, Bill
    Chipper Jones / Bill Zack; introduction by Jim Murray;
  senior consultant, Earl Weaver.
        64 p.   cm.—(Baseball legends)
    Includes bibliographical references (p. 62) and index.
    Summary: A biography of the All-Star player who is the
  third baseman for the Atlanta Braves.
    ISBN 0-7910-5157-9
    1. Jones, Chipper, 1972– —Juvenile literature. 2. Baseball players—
  United States—Biography—Juvenile literature.
  [1. Jones, Chipper, 1972– . 2. Baseball players.] I. Weaver, Earl, 1930– .
  II. Title. III. Series
  GV865.J633Z33 1999
  796.357'092—dc21
  (B)   99-12001
                                                                      CIP

CONTENTS

WHAT MAKES A STAR

Jim Murray

No one has ever been able to explain to me the mysterious alchemy that makes one man a .350 hitter and another player, more or less identical in physical makeup, hard put to hit .200. You look at an Al Kaline, who played with the Detroit Tigers from 1953 to 1974. He was pale, stringy, almost poetic-looking. He always seemed to be struggling against a bad case of mononucleosis. But with a bat in his hands, he was King Kong. During his career, he hit 399 home runs, rapped out 3,007 hits, and compiled a .297 batting average.

Form isn't the reason. The first time anybody saw Roberto Clemente step into the batter's box for the Pittsburgh Pirates, the best guess was that Clemente would be back in Double A ball in a week. He had one foot in the bucket and held his bat at an awkward angle—he looked as though he couldn't hit an outside pitch. A lot of other ballplayers may have had a better-looking stance. Yet they never led the National League in hitting in four different years, the way Clemente did.

Not every ballplayer is born with the ability to hit a curveball. Nor is exceptional hand-eye coordination the key to heavy hitting. Big league locker rooms are filled with players who have all the attributes, save one: discipline. Every baseball man can tell you a story about a pitcher who throws a ball faster than anyone has ever seen but who has no control on or *off* the field.

The Hall of Fame is full of people who transformed themselves into great ballplayers by working at the sport, by studying the game, and making sacrifices. They're overachievers—and winners. If you want to find them, just watch the World Series. Or simply read about New York Yankee great Lou Gehrig; Ted Williams, "the Splendid Splinter" of the Boston Red Sox; or the Dodgers' strikeout king, Sandy Koufax.

A pitcher *should* be able to win a lot of ballgames with a 98-miles-per-hour fastball. But what about the pitcher who wins 20 games a year with a fastball so slow that you can catch it with your teeth? Bob Feller of the Cleveland Indians got into the Hall of Fame with a blazing fastball that glowed in the dark. National League star Grover Cleveland Alexander got there with a pitch that took considerably longer to reach the plate; but when it did arrive, the pitch was exactly where Alexander wanted it to be— and the last place the batter expected it to be.

There are probably more players with exceptional ability who didn't make it to the major leagues than there are who did. A number of great hitters, bored with fielding practice, had to be dropped from their team because their home-run production didn't make up for their lapses in the field. And then there are players like Brooks Robinson of the Baltimore Orioles, who made himself into a human vacuum cleaner at third base because he knew that working hard to become an expert fielder would win him a job in the big leagues.

A star is not something that flashes through the sky. That's a comet. Or a meteor. A star is something you can steer ships by. It stays in place and gives off a steady glow; it is fixed, permanent. A star works at being a star.

And that's how you tell a star in baseball. He shows up night after night and takes pride in how brightly he shines. He's Willie Mays running so hard his hat keeps falling off; Ty Cobb sliding to stretch a single into a double; Lou Gehrig, after being fooled in his first two at-bats, belting the next pitch off the light tower because he's taken the time to study the pitcher. Stars never take themselves for granted. That's why they're stars.

1

WINNING IT ALL

It was the top of the ninth inning and the Atlanta Braves needed one more out to win the 1995 World Series. Third baseman Chipper Jones watched Cleveland Indians second baseman Carlos Baerga approach home plate and get ready to hit.

"If he hits it to me," Jones said to himself, "I'll catch it."

But when Baerga hit the ball, it sailed over Jones's head into left center field. He turned and watched as center fielder Marquis Grissom chased it. As the ball settled in Grissom's glove, Jones raised his arms, shouted with happiness, and jumped on top of the pile of players celebrating on the infield grass.

"There was a lot of disbelief on my part," Jones said. "It was my first year and it was a feeling like, I can't believe this is happening. I had come so far the year before, not being able to play, and then winning a World Series, it was sweet, to say the least. I don't think even if you tried, you could do it justice."

The 23-year-old Jones had missed the entire 1994 season after suffering a serious knee injury during spring training. In 1995, his first season

Chipper Jones's athletic ability enables him to play more than one position; he has never hesitated to switch when asked by the Braves.

in the major leagues, he led all rookies with 86 RBI and runs scored with 87, and was second with 23 home runs and 139 hits.

It hadn't taken him long to prove he was an outstanding player. Manager Bobby Cox batted him in the key third spot in the Braves' lineup and twice asked him to change positions. A natural shortstop, Jones was switched in spring training to third base, a very difficult transition for most shortstops. Then, when Ryan Klesko was put on the 15-day disabled list in May, Jones moved to left field and performed flawlessly.

"He could play anywhere," Cox said. "And you wouldn't even have to ask him. If we have a hole somewhere, he'll volunteer to play there."

Perhaps most impressively, Jones lived up to all the hype surrounding him.

"He is," Atlanta general manager John Schuerholz said, "pretty remarkable."

Teammate Mark Wohlers called Jones a special player. Cox predicted he would become a perennial All-Star and made comparisons to Braves Hall of Fame third baseman Eddie Mathews.

It was a season Jones would never forget, starting with the three game-winning home runs he hit during the regular season. His ninth-inning home run against the Colorado Rockies in Game 1 of the division series lifted the Braves to a 5–4 victory.

Then came the National League Championship Series (NLCS) against the Cincinnati Reds. Jones helped the Braves win four straight games by hitting .438 and driving in three runs. The World Series was next and Atlanta was ready to celebrate its first world championship after losing to the Minnesota Twins in 1991 and the Toronto Blue Jays in 1992.

Larry Jones, Chipper's father, says Chipper's greatest attribute is not his natural swing, his base-running instincts, or his solid defense.

"He's always been an extremely hard worker," Larry Jones said. "He will compete with you in dominoes, Scrabble, gin rummy just like he's playing the seventh game of the World Series. His work ethic and his competitiveness probably do more for him than his natural ability."

Chipper Jones knew he would play in the major leagues someday when he was still playing Little League. He practiced more than the other

Jones is congratulated by second baseman Mark Lemke after his two-run homer in Game 3 of the 1995 NLCS. The Braves swept Cincinnati to advance to the World Series.

Rookie Chipper Jones reaches the mound just after Atlanta catcher Javy Lopez leaps into the arms of pitcher Mark Wohlers after the Braves won the 1995 World Series against the Cleveland Indians.

kids and was willing to work harder than anyone else to meet his goals.

"I remember having goals when I was eight," Jones said. "While it may not have been as high as I am right now, my sights when I was eight were to play in the major division of our Little League, play with the 11- and 12-year-olds. I think every year or two you graduate up to another goal. When I was eight years old, that was my first year of organized baseball, so I wanted to make that team and make a contribution. I was serious about it. You're talking about a guy who came from a baseball family, so baseball wasn't taken too lightly."

The same approach allowed him to move through five minor league stops and make it to the major leagues in a little more than three years.

"I'm a bit of a perfectionist," he said. "I'm always picking at what's wrong and trying to correct it so that my game will be flawless. I'm looking for that point in my game where I'm hitting .300 from both sides of the plate with power, I'm driving in runs, and I'm playing flawless defense."

"What can one say about the Chipper?" Cox asked. "His attitude is, 'Whatever's best for the team.' Where does it come from? Look at his family. Good people, his mother and his father. His father's a baseball coach. Good man."

That explains how a kid from a town that has one stoplight could handle the pressure of big games in the postseason with unflappable cool. Against the Indians, he looked like a player who had been to 10 World Series, not just one.

"I've been through a lot of pressure games in my life," Jones said. "Some guys live for crunch time. I'm one of them."

Several days after the Braves celebrated the first World Series championship in Atlanta history, Jones rode on top of a truck carrying the team down Peachtree Street as fans cheered and confetti drifted down through the cool October air. He waved and saluted the 750,000 fans who lined the parade route until his arm became so tired he started waving with his left hand.

"It was the greatest feeling in the world," Jones said. "It's something I'll never forget. I couldn't have asked for a better first season in the major leagues."

2

BORN TO PLAY BALL

L arry Wayne Jones Jr., known as Chipper, was born on April 24, 1972 in Deland, Florida, near the family ranch in Pierson. His father was a baseball coach at Pierson Taylor High School.

Starting when he was six, Chipper and his father would go out between the barn and the carport and fire tennis balls at each other from 40 feet away. At first, Chipper wasn't strong enough to swing a regular bat, so his father cut a length of PVC pipe for a bat. It wasn't long before Chipper became so good with the pipe, he switched to a Louisville Slugger.

"That's how I learned how to hit," Jones said. "That's probably why I'm such a good fastball hitter."

The backyard is also where Chipper learned to switch-hit. Though his father was a Dodgers fan, his favorite player was Mickey Mantle, so he taught his son how to switch-hit, just like Mickey. Very soon Chipper was hitting balls right-handed and left-handed over the hay barn.

When his father was busy coaching his team, Chipper would spend hours in the backyard, bouncing tennis balls off the house and roof so

Expected to be a first-round pick in the 1990 draft, Chipper Jones posed wearing the caps of the first six teams to make their choices. Atlanta made him the No. 1 selection in the country.

he could practice his fielding. He always described the action, just like a play-by-play announcer.

"That's probably why he's good on the radio," his mother, Lynne, said. "He was out there playing by himself, carrying on a running commentary. I know lots of kids do it, but he did it constantly."

Baseball was the primary subject spoken about in the Jones house. Chipper and his father were constantly discussing the game, the greatest players of all time, and who was the Dodgers' best player. Although Chipper played football in high school, his first love remained baseball.

"When you grow up in a baseball family," he said, "all you're talking about at the dinner table, on the ride to school, it was always baseball."

When he was young, Larry Jr. was given the nickname Chipper because all his relatives thought he resembled his father. Thus, he was "a chip off the old block." The nickname stuck.

"Chipper and his father are absolute clones," Lynne said. "They stand the same way, they walk the same, they field the same. Watching Chipper play shortstop in high school was like watching Larry play shortstop in college. They are both competitive—to a fault. When Chipper comes home and wants his father to throw him a little batting practice, the next thing you know, Larry's trying to strike him out and Chipper's trying to hit home runs. But that's what makes them so good at what they do."

"Chipper is a good name," Jones said. "If I was called Larry Jones, who'd remember that? Chipper is one of those first names people remember. Think of Cal or Mickey. You hear those names and you say, 'Those were some of the best to ever play the game.' I'd like to be thought of like that someday."

Even as a boy, Chipper dreamed of playing in the major leagues.

"I wanted to be a major league baseball player from day one," he said.

When he was 12, Chipper began to dominate Little League, hitting three home runs in a game against an Altamonte Springs team that went on to the Little League World Series.

"It was kinda scary, but I said to my wife that day that I think he might be one of the 10 best players in his age group in the country," Larry Jones said. "She said, 'You're just a Little League dad talking.' But we kid about it now and I say, 'I told you so.'"

Chipper was cool as frost; pressure never fazed him. As a seventh-grader playing on the Pierson Taylor JV basketball team, he was fouled with three seconds remaining, his team trailing by a point, and a hostile crowd screaming. The referee handed him the ball. Chipper tucked it underneath his arm and waved to the fans to scream louder.

"I thought, 'What a hot dog,'" Larry Jones said.

Chipper calmly sank both foul shots to win the game. Afterward his father asked, "Why do you put that kind of pressure on yourself?"

Chipper responded, "I was going to make 'em."

"When the rest of us turn to Jell-O, he turns it on," Lynne said. "It never ceases to amaze me."

Some people might say Chipper was cocky, but he described his attitude on the field as one of confidence, something his mother, a champion equestrian rider and trainer, taught him at a young age.

"My mom instilled in me early that you need a necessary arrogance to be able to compete, especially in this game," Jones said. "She always

Jones pitched and played shortstop for the Bolles Bulldogs in Jacksonville, Florida, where he was also an All-State wide receiver and avid golfer.

taught me to have that little strut about you, that little swagger that says, 'You may get me this time, but I'm going to get you back seven-fold the next.' She was always like, 'Don't you ever, ever let any pitcher know that he's got you. Even if he strikes you out, you walk back to the dugout and if you've got to talk a little smack to him, talk a little smack.' Whenever I need a pep talk, she's always there to kick me in the butt and get me back on track with the mental part. Most guys, when their mom suggests something, roll their eyes. When my mom does, I listen. She's a tough little lady."

But Chipper's air of confidence sometimes deserted him. Whenever he faced a bigger challenge—a higher level of competition, like going from Little League to Babe Ruth and then to high school—he felt unsure of himself until he could prove that he belonged.

When he was 14, Chipper Jones played second base on the varsity high school team. He was in eighth grade.

"You're talking about a 14-year-old playing varsity baseball with 17- and 18-year-olds," Jones said. "I started to realize there weren't a tremendous amount of eighth-graders who make a varsity team."

Larry Jones decided things were too easy for Chipper at Pierson Taylor. "He was catching a break at school because I worked there and he was an athlete," Larry said.

"He was making straight A's and he never cracked a book," Lynne said.

They sent Chipper to The Bolles School, a prestigious boarding school 90 miles away in Jacksonville, for the 10th grade.

"I went from being a big fish in a little pond to a little fish in a big ol' lake," Chipper said. "It was tough, a big growing-up process. You're talking about a little country hick from a one-stoplight town going to the big city and pulling into a parking lot full of better cars than I drove, and a lot of rich kids. I didn't really fit in. I had problems. But the first time they saw me swing a bat, I made a few friends."

For the next three years Chipper found himself playing against his old school in the state playoffs. Each time Bolles beat Pierson.

"That was tough," he said. "I couldn't go away to another school, come back and lose. That was the most pressure I'd ever felt. People have always expected big things of Chipper Jones. And I've always answered the bell."

Bolles rolled up a 66–19 record during Chipper's three years, going to the state finals twice and winning one championship. In addition to batting .488 in his senior year, the 6'3", 185-pound Jones had a 7–2 record as a pitcher with a 1.00 ERA. But most big league teams were not interested in him as a pitcher. They saw him as a potential all-star shortstop.

As a wide receiver, Chipper was named to the first-team all-state football team in his senior year. That brought him scholarship offers from UCLA, USC, and Stanford when he graduated in 1990. The University of Miami wanted him to play college baseball for them.

The Atlanta Braves had scouted Chipper as intently as any big league team. Bobby Cox, then the general manager, had gone to Jacksonville to see him play in the spring. "We had at least 10 [scouts] look at him," Cox said, "and everything came back positive."

The Braves were especially impressed with Chipper's switch-hitting and his speed; he had stolen 48 bases in 50 attempts in three seasons.

But Jones was not the Braves' first choice. They were eager to draft Texas high school pitcher Todd Van Poppel, until they became convinced that Van Poppel was going to play at the University of Texas and would not sign with anybody who drafted him.

Since Chipper had signed a letter of intent to go to Miami, a Braves scout visited the Jones home in Pierson on the Sunday before the draft to ask if he would indeed sign with whoever drafted him. Larry Jones assured him that Chipper wanted to play ball if he received a fair bonus.

The Braves would pick first because they had finished with the worst record in the National League in 1989. On the day of the draft—Monday, June 4—the Jones home was filled with more than 30 members of the family and friends waiting for a phone call from somebody. Chipper confidently expected to be among the top five or six players chosen. He leaned toward the Braves because most of their farm teams were in the south, but he just wanted to get started on his career, whoever drafted him.

When the phone rang a little after noon, Chipper answered it. He heard the words "Atlanta Braves" and got goosebumps. He had been picked number one in the country. He hung up, grinned, and made a two-thumbs-up gesture that said it all.

Later he could not recall anything else that had been said nor the name of the person who had called.

Chipper's coach at Bolles, Don Suriano, was proud to have coached the first top draft pick to come out of Florida. "This is something a coach dreams about, to work with a kid like this."

That afternoon a Braves scout came to the house. Chipper's father did the negotiating, which didn't take long. Once he and Chipper left the room to talk.

Chipper knew he had to prove himself every time he advanced in baseball, but he never lacked self-confidence. He credits his mother with instilling in him the "necessary arrogance to be able to compete."

"Chipper, you can get more than [they are offering]," Jones said.

"I know, but I want to be playing in a week," Chipper replied.

They walked back into the room. His father said to the scout, "If you'll meet us halfway, you have a deal."

Jones signed for a $350,000 bonus, a record for a high school player.

As eager as he was to begin his professional career, Chipper realized that he was facing his biggest jump in competition. Being a number one draft choice does not automatically guarantee success; about half the highly touted top selections fail to make it to the major leagues.

In the minor leagues Chipper would find that he was an even smaller fish in a bigger lake than he had been when he transferred to Bolles. It is common for a minor league team to have a dozen all-staters and a few college stars on the roster, competing for the shrinking number of spots as they climb the ladder to the majors. He would learn that playing every day, sometimes after long bus rides, was a far harder grind than the short high school season, and he would be playing in front of crowds of strangers, instead of family and friends.

But none of that daunted Chipper on this happy day. "I'm on top of the world," he said, "but I'm glad it's over. Now I'm ready to play ball. I asked the Braves how long it might take me to move up and they said it's entirely up to me. It all comes down to my performance."

3

SUCCESS AND DISASTER

Chipper Jones didn't have to go very far to begin his pro career. He drove across Florida to Bradenton, a small town on the Gulf of Mexico, and reported to the Braves' club in the rookie Gulf Coast League. The adjustment to living on his own wasn't difficult because he had been away from home since he was 15. But a broken hand suffered in a fight with a teammate at Bolles two weeks before the draft slowed his progress; he finished with a .229 average and hit only one home run in 44 games.

It was a difficult time for Jones, and he grew so despondent over his failure to hit that he considered giving up switch-hitting.

Braves third base coach Bobby Dews was the organization's farm director at the time. When the Bradenton manager told him Jones was thinking about hitting strictly right-handed, Dews called Braves scouting director Paul Snyder.

"Paul told me he didn't think it would be a real good thing if [Jones quit switch-hitting]," Dews said. "He told me if Jones quit switch-hitting, the manager in Bradenton's going to lose his job. And

Jones considered shortstop his natural position, but he played some second base in the minors. He also played the outfield before the Braves moved him to third base.

Jones rose rapidly through the Atlanta farm system, setting records and living up to the Braves' expectations at every level. Three years after leaving high school he collected his first major league hit.

you're probably going to lose yours, too. It wasn't much of a decision after that."

Jones continued switch-hitting and returned home following the season determined to work even harder to reach his goal.

"I read the papers, read what people were saying about me, that the Braves made a mistake in selecting me," he said. "It kind of ticked me off. The only way to make those people eat a little crow was work my butt off."

Jones's hard work paid off in 1991 when he was selected as the starting shortstop for the Class A South Atlantic League All-Star Game and was named the league's most outstanding major league prospect after hitting .326 with 15 home runs and 98 RBI for Macon.

Another significant event happened in Macon that helped change his life. He met Karin (pronounced CAR-in) Fulford, who was an early childhood education major at nearby Wesleyan College. The pair fell in love and were married following the 1992 season.

Jones's rise up the minor league ladder began in earnest in 1992 when he started at Class A Durham and hit .277, then was promoted to Greenville in the Class AA Southern League, where he batted .346 and set a club record with 11 triples. Twice he was named the league's Player of the Week; the league managers named him their top prospect.

In 1993 he led the AAA International League in hits, runs, total bases, and triples, while batting .325 at Richmond. He was named Richmond's Most Valuable Player (MVP) and was selected as the league's Rookie of the Year.

On September 10, he was called up by the Braves and four days later got his first hit in his first at-bat against the Reds.

"I walked up to the plate and I couldn't feel my arms and I couldn't feel my legs," Jones remembered. "I got a warm reception from the fans in Atlanta, then it was all a blur. The pitcher threw a fastball and I got a swinging bunt hit down the third base line. I felt a tremendous amount of relief that I was finally in the big leagues and I had got a hit in my first at-bat."

When Jones walked into the Braves' clubhouse at West Palm Beach the following February for the start of spring training, he knew there was a problem. The incumbent shortstop was Jeff Blauser, who had hit .305 and driven in 73 runs in 1993, which meant Jones had to find another position. Anxious to get his bat into the lineup, manager Bobby Cox solved the dilemma by asking Jones to learn to play left field.

Although Jones had played shortstop his entire career, he accepted the challenge eagerly, and within a matter of days he proved he was a natural outfielder. Cox planned to have Jones in the lineup as the starting left fielder on opening day when disaster struck.

Running toward first base in a spring training game against the Yankees, Jones twisted to avoid a tag. "I planted my left foot to jump to the outside," Jones remembered. "When I planted, my spike caught and my knee just kept going to the outside. I felt a pop, like the bottom half of my knee was pointing outward. It was a real bad burning pain for about five minutes. Then it went away."

Jones had torn a ligament in his left knee. A serious knee injury has ended many an athlete's career. Suddenly Jones's big league dreams were threatened.

The season started without Jones in the lineup. He underwent reconstructive surgery two weeks later, and doctors predicted it would take him a year to recover completely. It was a devastating blow to the 21-year-old. Every time he saw a Braves commercial on TV, he was reminded of what he was missing.

"It kind of gets me in the dumps when I see that," he said. "I don't really want to talk to anybody right now because it makes me remember what I'm missing, what I could be doing."

Soon he rejoined the team and though it was difficult to watch the season unfold without him, he continued his exercises and dreamed of the day he would return to the field.

"Obviously I felt like I had done enough to make the club," he said. "I was a little down the first night, but I realize it's not going to get any better unless you work at it. No reason to dwell on it."

He bristled when it was suggested he might not be the same player again and vowed to return as good as new. "All I can say is if [the fans] doubt me coming back, they don't know me real well," he said. "They may think I'm going to lose a step or it will affect me mentally, but I don't see why the Braves shouldn't get the old Chipper Jones back."

Doctors told him nine months was the minimum amount of time required to recover from the injury. Most athletes need between nine months and one year to fully recuperate following this type of surgery. Jones quietly told his doctors he planned to be playing again by September.

"I'm dead serious," he said. "I've told them that I'm not an average human being. I consider myself a world-class athlete. I'm not like everyone else. I've always had good work habits and really earned what I got."

He began strengthening his knee and maintaining his overall condition by pedaling a

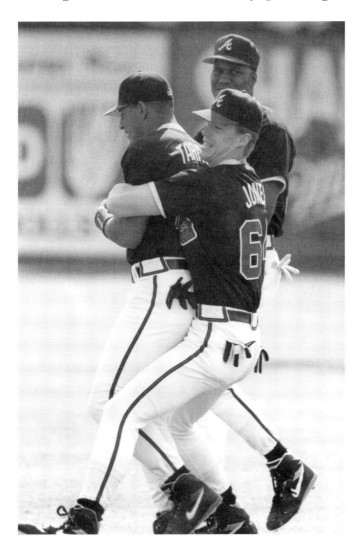

Invited to the Braves' spring training camp in 1993, Jones enjoyed some horseplay with Tony Tarasco, a '92 teammate at Greenville. Jones went to Richmond for the '93 season and was the International League Rookie of the Year.

stationary bicycle, followed by a rigorous work-out on a StairMaster. In the first five weeks following his surgery, doctors were astonished to see a recovery they normally would see in three months after the operation.

"Before the surgery I saw what that kind of injury did to the average person," Jones said. "It was a bit scary seeing people two months after their surgery not even off crutches. That made me work that much harder."

During games he sat alone in the players' lounge and watched on television as his team-mates played without him. With a sound like a distant rumble of thunder, he could hear the roar of the crowd and feel the stadium shake with the fans' excitement. The scar on his left knee was a constant reminder that he couldn't be on the field with his fellow rookies, Ryan Klesko and Javy Lopez.

"It's killing me," Jones said. "It's torture. If you want to torture me, blow my knee out and let me watch these guys play. I used to be really depressed when I went 0-for-4 and made an error. I'd love to do that now."

Jones began swinging a bat again in mid-June. He was making remarkable progress when suddenly major league players went on strike in August. The season was over. Jones, who was making the minimum salary of $109,000, stopped receiving a paycheck. There were pay-ments on the house he and Karin had bought in Atlanta, car payments, and credit cards to pay off—and no money.

"Chipper's heart beats for baseball," Karin remembered, "and in 1994 he lost baseball two ways. He had an injury that made him realize that you never know when the game is going to be taken away from you. And then the strike. We were two months away from having to sell our house. I took a job as a substitute teacher. Then in that same year, my parents got divorced. We cried a lot, and we prayed a lot."

Said Chipper, "There was a pretty severe period of depression there for a little while. My whole life had revolved around baseball and now it was being taken away from me. It made me sit back and think about things a little bit. I'm glad I went through it because it's good to struggle sometimes."

A ROOKIE IN THE WORLD SERIES

After a year of rehabilitation and hard work, Chipper Jones was ready to resume his major league career in 1995. But when he arrived at spring training, he was again asked to learn a new position. The Braves had a left fielder in Ryan Klesko, but with Terry Pendleton's departure, they were without a third baseman. Jones agreed to return to the infield and begin his rookie season in the position popularly known as "the hot corner."

It turned out to be a difficult transition. He committed 25 errors, second among National League third basemen to San Diego's Ken Caminiti, though many of those misplays occurred during the final month of the season.

"I was happy with my defense until the last month," Jones said. "When we clinched, my concentration sort of went out the window and it escalated from there." In his first 113 games, from the start of the season until August 31, he made only 14 errors. During the final month, with the pennant race over, he was charged with 11 errors in 27 games.

There was no question in the Braves' minds that Jones could play third base. Only Caminiti, Philadelphia's Charlie Hayes, and Florida's Terry Pendleton handled more fielding chances than Jones. If he had maintained his concentration in September, he probably would have finished with about 18 errors and been a Gold Glove candidate.

"He was an above-average third baseman," Cox said. "I think someday he'll be an All-Star and maybe win a Gold Glove."

For a player who spent his career at shortstop, Jones made the move to third look easy. There wasn't a third baseman in the league who charged a bunt and made an off-balance throw to first better than he did.

"For a guy who's played there only one year," Atlanta pitcher Tom Glavine said after the season, "he's not that far from being as good as Terry Pendleton and Matt Williams. He did a heck of a job handling it all and he's only going to get better."

Though third base remained Jones's position, he also played 20 games in the outfield without an error. He preferred to return there, but with a crop of young outfielders coming up from the minors and no other third baseman, his days in the outfield appeared numbered.

"I love playing the outfield," he said. "It's so much less pressure than third base. But we've got a lot of great athletes who can play the outfield, and not a lot who can play third base."

While Jones was proving he could handle third base, he also showed he was a natural leader. When the club was in the midst of a five-game losing streak, he called for a team meeting to clear the air.

"Maybe we need to get into a brawl or something to take out our frustrations," he said. "I do say that in jest. But there are a lot of people frustrated. We don't have a lot of vocal leaders in here. We haven't had a team meeting called by a player. We need a kick in the butt. I don't think we have played a solid nine innings more than one or two times all year."

Jones was a natural leader on the field, too. With him in the lineup, the Braves put together the greatest season in Atlanta history. Jones hit

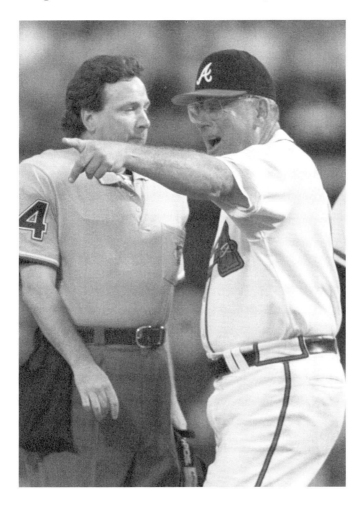

Atlanta manager Bobby Cox had no doubts that Jones had the athletic ability to play anywhere he was asked. Cox often had more doubts about the correctness of some umpires' calls.

Cal Ripken Jr., who had just broken Lou Gehrig's record of 2,130 consecutive games, was invited to throw out the first ball to start the 1995 World Series. Jones asked to meet him and came away with a signed ball.

.265 with 23 home runs and 86 RBI and led all major league rookies in six offensive categories. He was disappointed when Dodgers pitcher Hideo Nomo edged him out for Rookie of the Year. The Japanese right-hander led the league with 236 strikeouts while winning 13 against 6 losses.

"Maybe sometimes the best guy doesn't always win," he said. "I sort of prepared myself for the worst. I told everyone close to me not to get their hopes up." Jones got some satisfaction from being named Rookie of the Year by *The Sporting News* in balloting by National League players.

Jones saved his best performances for October. In Game 1 of the Division Series against the Colorado Rockies, he hit a pair of home runs, the last one coming in the ninth inning with the game tied 4–4. But he had saved the game for the Braves the inning before when he dove onto his belly, made a brilliant backhand grab of Andres Galarraga's smash, and threw to second to get a force-out.

Jones remembered reacting to the ball instinctively. "It was just a reaction play. I saw it was an off-speed pitch and I was leaning (toward the line). Lucky enough it stuck in my glove."

Rockies manager Don Baylor said, "That play was probably the game-winner. Then Chipper came back and hit the game-winner."

When Jones made the diving play, he twisted his left knee, and it was throbbing when he went up to bat in the ninth inning. So the last thing he expected to do was hit a home run.

"It was like I was two feet off the ground," he recalled. "A big adrenaline rush."

In Game 2, Atlanta was behind 4–3 in the ninth when Jones led off with a double, starting a rally that sent the Braves to a 7–4 victory. In Game 4 he had another huge hit. Atlanta trailed 3-0 with two on and two out in the third when Jones doubled home two runs. Fred McGriff followed with a two-run homer and the Braves never trailed again, going on to win 10–4. Despite playing with a sore left knee and an aching back, Jones batted .389 with two homers, four RBI, and outstanding defense.

"Every time I see him he impresses me more," Rockies shortstop Walt Weiss said.

After Jones hit .438 with one homer and three RBI to lead the Braves to a four-game sweep of the Reds in the NLCS, Cincinnati manager Davey Johnson said, "He handles himself like he's been around a lot longer than his first year."

Some Hall of Famers finish their careers without ever playing in a World Series. Reaching that goal in his rookie season was a dream come true for Jones. "He came out of the clubhouse after they clinched against the Reds," Larry Jones remembered, "and he whispered in my ear, 'Dad! Can you believe I'm going to play in a World Series. It's just like a dream.'"

Jones was asked before the World Series started whether there was anything about the postseason he was not enjoying. "Not one second hasn't been fun," he answered.

Jones had always idolized Baltimore Orioles shortstop Cal Ripken Jr., so when the legendary player threw out the first ball at Game 1, Jones asked to meet him. Ripken signed a ball for him. The inscription read, "Chipper, your career is off to a great start. Now comes the hard part."

The Braves had the next to lowest team batting average on the National League. Four men hit over 20 home runs each, but they had no 50-homer or big RBI slugger. They depended on pitching and defense to win. Their pitching staff had the lowest ERA in the league for the third straight year.

Their World Series opponents, the Cleveland Indians, had baseball's best-hitting team in a generation, led by Albert Belle. They were also a loud, belligerent team, popping off and taunting the Braves as underachievers. Pitcher Orel Hershiser said, "Atlanta feels pressure from not winning the 1991 and '92 World Series." Belle blasted reporters and photographers, chasing them out of the dugout and away from the batting cage. DH Eddie Murray was the opposite, refusing to talk to anyone.

The Braves were content to say, "Good pitching will beat good hitting," and went out and proved it. They took a three-games-to-two lead, but that didn't stop the Indians from keeping up the banter. When Indians shortstop Omar Vizquel said, "They know they can't win a World Series," Atlanta pitcher Tommy Glavine said, "That statement made me madder than anything else."

The Braves called a team meeting before Game 6. "We were a little concerned about it," Glavine said, "and a couple guys got up and said it didn't matter what they said. We controlled the Series, and if we just played our game we'd win it."

Then he went out and pitched a one-hit shutout for eight innings. Mark Wohlers pitched the ninth. Braves outfielder David Justice's home run produced the only run in Atlanta's World Series clincher.

In postseason play, Chipper Jones set rookie records with 19 hits and three home runs.

As they celebrated in Atlanta-Fulton County Stadium, a new stadium was under construction nearby for the 1996 Olympics. In 1997 it would become Turner Field, the new home of the Braves, and Atlanta's first world championship banner would fly over it.

5

FALLING SHORT

In the spring of 1996, Chipper Jones became a millionaire. He signed a four-year contract for $8.25 million, with an option for a fifth year that could make the deal worth up to $13.5 million.

"The Braves have offered me some stability for the next five years and I'm extremely happy," he said. "It's something I really didn't expect. Not many young players get this type of offer. For them to come to me is quite a compliment."

The Braves broke with tradition to sign Jones to the contract. In the past the club had been reluctant to give multi-year deals to young players.

"Chipper is the kind of guy who we're going to have to build the nucleus of the Braves around," general manager John Schuerholz said. "It's very fitting that he's the first young guy that this organization made a policy change for."

Some players, including several teammates, were critical of Jones for his contract. They told him that if he had waited and continued to be successful, he could have received much more money.

"When I hear that, I just laugh in their faces," Jones said. "I don't play baseball for money; I play

Jones snags a shot by Yankee shortstop Derek Jeter in Game 5 of the 1996 World Series. After winning the first two games, Atlanta lost the next four.

for love of the game. I have no desire to be the highest-paid player. I'm happy with my life."

He celebrated his new wealth with his best season, becoming the first Brave since Dale Murphy in 1985 to hit over .300, with 30 homers, 110 RBI, and 114 runs. He was also selected to his first All-Star team and started at third base in place of the injured Matt Williams.

During the season Jones got into trouble with his teammates during a three-week road trip while the Olympics were held in Atlanta. The team lost three games in a row and Jones, who was writing a column for the local newspaper, said, "I don't like the way some people are going about their business."

Those were critical words from a second-year player and he soon regretted them.

"I knew the next morning I shouldn't have said that," Jones admitted. "Nobody said anything to me; nobody needed to. I just regretted it. I was frustrated when I said it. But what happens in the clubhouse should stay in the clubhouse. I made a mistake."

It was a measure of Jones's maturity that he admitted his mistake. His teammates forgave him.

"I think if you read the paper and read all the magazines and read everything they say about yourself, I think you make a lot of enemies," pitcher Greg Maddux said. "It becomes easy to forget that maybe the guys around you are just doing their jobs too and it becomes real easy to take it personally."

Once again the Braves won their division and swept through the playoffs. Jones hit only .222 in a three-game sweep of the Dodgers in the division series, but against the Cardinals in the NLCS, he tied a record with four hits in Game 1 and

batted .440 with four RBI. The Braves came back from being down three games to one to win the NLCS and go to their second straight World Series.

This time they returned home disappointed. After winning the first two games against the New York Yankees, they lost the next four. Jones hit a respectable .286, but all three of his RBI came in a 12–1 rout in Game 1.

"I felt like we were in total control in the first two games," he said. "I didn't feel that way in the last four."

Jones had another outstanding season in 1997, hitting .295 with 21 homers and a career-high 111 RBI. The Braves won the NL East again and swept the Houston Astros in the Division Series. For Atlanta, it was a record sixth straight NLCS appearance.

The Florida Marlins, in only their fifth year of existence, had earned the wild card spot

It didn't take long for Jones to display the instincts needed to become a Gold Glove third baseman. Here he snares a line drive and touches third for an out in the '96 World Series.

in the playoffs. They swept the San Francisco Giants to advance to the championship series, where they were given little chance to upset the pitching-rich Braves.

In the series opener in Atlanta, half of the Braves' pitching-and-defense formula failed them. Two errors resulted in five unearned runs and a 5–3 win for Florida over Greg Maddux. Chipper Jones contributed to the defensive lapses when he failed to stop Moises Alou's hopper down the line that became a three-run double in the first inning. He also homered in the losing cause.

Tommy Glavine's three-hitter evened the series; Jones homered again in the 7–1 win.

In Game 3 in Florida, Jones made an uncharacteristic baserunning mistake that marred a budding Braves rally. Leading 2–1 in the top of the sixth, Atlanta had Jeff Blauser on second and Jones on first with no outs. Fred McGriff singled to right. Jones, thinking Blauser would try to score on the hit, rounded second and headed for third. But Blauser stopped at third base. Jones was hung up and tagged out. After the game, manager Bobby Cox said, "It was just over-aggressiveness [on Chipper's part], I guess."

Florida scored four in the last of the sixth, aided by outfielder Andruw Jones misplaying a line drive, and won, 5–2.

To his own amazement and disgust, Chipper made an identical baserunning mistake in Game 4, but this time it did not affect the result, as Denny Neagle pitched a four-hitter for a 4–0 win to even the series.

Later, an embarrassed Jones said, "That probably gets me more than anything. You're going to make errors and I realize that. Yeah, I should have kept [Alou's] ball in the infield [in Game 1].

Whether I make the play or don't make the play, only one run should have scored. Those three runs set the tone of the series.

"But the baserunning really got to me, because not only did I mess up doing something that comes so naturally to me and I'm so good at. Not only did I mess up once. I turned around on the exact same play the next night and did the same thing. It was something weird. It was like an out-of-body experience. I was looking down on this guy and he's messing up time and time again."

The next night Greg Maddux pitched against Livan Hernandez, a veteran Cuban pitcher who had escaped from Cuba while his national team was in Mexico in 1995. The winner of Game 3, Hernandez gave up a leadoff triple to Kenny Lofton in the first inning, then walked Keith Lockhart. He then struck out Chipper Jones, Fred McGriff, and Ryan Klesko. That was the start of a pitchers' duel in which Hernandez struck out an LCS-record 15, and Greg Maddux gave up just three hits, but they were enough for the Marlins to edge the Braves, 2–1.

The Braves believed that home plate umpire Eric Gregg's wide strike zone was a factor in Hernandez's success against them. "I swung at pitches that were a foot outside," Jones said. "I turned around and asked if they were strikes, and he said yes. I couldn't help but give a little chuckle. I'm so mad I can't see straight."

Trailing three games to two, the Braves returned home for Game 6 and ran into a peevish and disappointed 50,446 fans. When Chipper Jones's name was announced, the boos from his home crowd rang in his ears. It was the first time he had incurred the wrath of fans and

Jones's father taught him to be a switch-hitter when he was in Little League. Through 1998 Chipper had hit for a higher average and more home runs from the left side.

it disturbed him. He understood their anger, but it was still a painful experience.

"I was disappointed in myself for those three mistakes," he said. "But if I had been in the stands I probably would have been booing too. They were sensing just what we were feeling, that frustration of it slipping away. I don't blame them."

In the clubhouse he remained confident despite being one loss away from elimination. "How many times have we won two in a row since we've been here?" he asked, knowing that it was something they had done plenty of times.

But not this time. The Marlins jumped on Tommy Glavine for four runs in the top of the first as an error by the shortstop on a double play ball proved costly. The Braves scored one in the first and two in the second to make it 4–3. Aided by several ground balls that bounced high off the rock-hard dirt in front of home plate, Florida scored three in the sixth and took a commanding 7–3 lead behind their ace, Kevin Brown. They had scored the seven runs on only four hits.

Chipper Jones had one more chance to be a hero and turn the crowd's boos into cheers. In the ninth, with the score 7–4, two men on base and two outs, he stepped intro the batter's box representing the tying run. He grounded to second for a force-out that ended their season.

The frustration of watching the Marlins advance to the World Series drove Jones into seclusion. He picked up his rifle and retreated to the woods, where he could hunt and reflect on the season's sour ending in private.

"I like to get away. I think that was really the first time in my life I've gone out of my way to avoid having to talk," he said. "I went through a period there where I didn't want to see my name in the paper. I was burned out. I didn't want to talk to anybody, I didn't want to even think about it. I wanted to rest my mind and my body and just meditate for a little while. I thought the healthiest thing for me was to just kind of get away, not talk about it, not think about it, and just recover."

More disappointment followed in 1998. Jones set career highs with a .313 batting average and 34 home runs, and the Braves won a franchise-record 106 games. But for the players and fans

Jones's speed helps him pick up infield hits, especially when batting from the left side.

of Atlanta, no season was a success unless they won it all.

They swept the Cubs in the Division Series and went into their seventh consecutive NLCS as heavy favorites over the NL West winners, the San Diego Padres. This time they got the pitching and defense, but they didn't hit. Jones was 5 for 24 with no home runs and only one RBI in the six games. Once again they lost the last game at home, managing just two hits in a 5–0 defeat. With just one world championship to show for their seven NLCS appearances, the Braves continued to bear the label of underachievers.

"It's tough to swallow," Jones said. "Wait 'til next year—we're saying it again this year. You swallow hard and go home."

Chipper Jones and the Braves went into 1999, Jones's last year of his four-year contract, expecting to continue to dominate the National League East, but with a lot still to prove to themselves and their fans.

6

THE PRICE OF FAME

It didn't take long for Chipper Jones to learn that being a star was not always fun. There were times when he became tired of all the attention. He signed autographs while eating dinner in a restaurant. He could not take a quiet walk with his wife without fans following them. He couldn't even watch a movie without interruption.

"There's been a couple of times when we've been sitting in a theater and had little kids running up and down the aisles trying to find me," he said.

Fame came with a high price tag. In Atlanta, Jones couldn't go out without being recognized. He was surrounded by fans wherever he went. The attention often kept him at home when he would have preferred to go out. Even at home he had no privacy. One day he was watching football on TV with his wife when 20 young girls came into his front yard and began chanting, "Chipper, we love you."

"Most of the kids who want my autograph aren't girls," Jones said. "There are some, but I would say the boys 10 to 12 years old are the majority—the ones just starting out in Little League and

Chipper Jones signs for fans at spring training in 1998. Hounded by autograph seekers wherever he goes, Jones and his wife find it difficult to enjoy any privacy outside their home.

starting to pay attention to games on TV for the first time."

Kids and their parents gathered outside the fence surrounding the players' parking lot at Turner Field and awaited his arrival. They leaned from the grandstand begging Jones to sign for them. Boxes of mail piled up in his locker in the clubhouse. If he were to sign every autograph requested of him, there would be no time to play ball.

Jones admired the way Cal Ripken Jr. stayed after spring training games for an hour to fill every request. "I have to applaud Ripken for all the autographs he signs. When you talk about the good guys in baseball, that's him. As much as I can, I try to be like that. But people have to

Often compared to former Braves third baseman Eddie Mathews (pictured here), a Hall of Famer who hit 512 home runs, Chipper Jones even resembles him physically.

realize we have a life outside baseball and a million things to do at home. Things go on at home and sometimes the most important thing is not signing your name."

Chippermania was everywhere. He became one of the game's most recognized stars. There were Chipper Jones posters, baseball cards, bats, and other merchandise. He did car commercials, talk shows, and radio spots. He even introduced the Chipper! candy bar, made by Malley's Chocolates of Cleveland.

"With a name like Chipper," said company president Dan Malley, "he was born to have a candy bar."

If he wanted to, Jones could make a personal appearance every day and still have a list of requests he couldn't fill. He found it difficult to say no to the dozens of invitations he received every month to speak at schools, churches, and youth groups, or appear at charity events, hospitals, and business meetings.

"At times it's tough on my family," Jones said. "I do get a lot of attention. There's a lot asked of me timewise and sometimes my family feels a little left out and that hurts my feelings a little bit. I can handle the popularity and the attention around the ballpark, but when it filters outside the ballpark and into my home and into a theater or restaurant, that's when it bothers me. If there was one thing that I could eliminate from being a professional ballplayer, it would be those distractions away from the field."

But Jones did not resent the adulation he received; he just tried to keep it in its place. "I don't consider being asked for autographs all the time to be the price to pay for fame. I consider it flattering. I still appreciate every kid who wants an autograph from me. I never envisioned I'd have the success or the popularity I have. I'm lucky because I play for a team with a superstation. All anybody has to do is turn on their TV at 7:30 every night to see us. I don't think it's just me they watch. There are a lot of

Jones is very particular about his bats, checking the grain of the wood closely to find the ones with the most hits in them.

players who are popular in this clubhouse. Deep down, I'll admit I never get tired of all the attention. I may get frustrated at it sometimes, but no matter who you are, you want the attention to be there. When they stop asking for autographs, that's when you're in trouble."

Keeping it all in its proper place was the difficult part. "From 2:00 P.M., when I arrive at the park for a night game, until I sign my last autograph after a game, I'm Chipper," he said. "The rest of the time I think of myself as Moe Jones, leading an ordinary upper-middle-class life."

Jones's future seemed unlimited.

"He reminds me so much of [Hall of Famer] Eddie Mathews," Bobby Cox said. "He plays like him, runs like him, even looks like him. He's in the elite category of players as far as I'm concerned."

Said Chipper, "People talk about having career years. I have yet to reach my career year. I'm a guy who's hit 30 home runs and driven in 110 runs, but I still don't think that's my career year. If I was to go 30–30, drive in 125 runs, win a Gold Glove, win a World Series on top of that, that would be a pretty good career year.

"Certainly, I'd like to have my name up there with Hank Aaron, Joe DiMaggio, Mickey Mantle. It's probably not going to happen, but if I have some championship rings under my belt and put up solid numbers for 15 to 20 years, people are going to look back and say Chipper Jones was a great player. He played on a great team, and this organization during the 1990s was one of the best that ever played the game."

While Jones became an idol to millions of kids playing baseball, he remained as down-to-earth as his roots in Pierson, Florida. Soon after he received his signing bonus in 1990, he donated part of it to fund construction of an office for his baseball coach at The Bolles School.

"It was kind of a payback to my coach and my school and baseball program for helping me out," he said. "We had a great field and cages and stuff, but we didn't have much of a locker room. My coach didn't have an office. I donated a little money so they can benefit."

In 1998 Jones was named the Braves' Man of the Year for his work in promoting good nutrition and exercise through the Big League Lunch Program, conducting clinics for kids, and raising money for cystic fibrosis research.

Chipper Jones paid particular attention to his bats, even counting the grains in the wood. Seventeen lines of grain was about right. Anything more or less indicated an inferior bat.

"I look for the thickness of the grain," he said. "It means the bat is less likely to flake. Usually the thick-grained bats are a little harder."

The first thing he did when he received a shipment of bats was check the grain, looking for five or six bats he could use in games. The remainder became batting practice bats.

"A good bat won't flake," he said. "Usually I've got two or three bats with me at any one time that I've had for a month or more. A bat is a player's baby. You find a good bat, it better not even be touched by another player."

Jones, a switch-hitter, used a lighter bat (33 ounces) from the right side than the left (34 ounces). He swung a black Glomar bat as a right-handed hitter and a white Rawlings bat from the left side.

After playing in three All-Star Games and two World Series, he still maintained the same work habits that brought him to the major leagues. He had become one of the best third basemen in the game and was among a handful of hitters pitchers feared the most.

Former Braves third baseman Terry Pendleton paid Jones the highest compliment when he said, "He shows up every day to win. He's going to get his work done, whatever it takes for him to be successful. I don't mean to knock the kids of today, but some of the kids, when they get to the big leagues, they just show up and they're happy to be here. He's not happy [just] to be in the big leagues. He works hard to stay here."

CHRONOLOGY

1972   Born in Pierson, Florida April 24.

1990   Number 1 draft pick by Atlanta Braves.
Signs for $350,000 bonus.

1991   Named top major league prospect in South Atlantic League.

1992   Marries Karin Fulford.

1993   Named International League Rookie of the Year at Richmond.
Gets a hit in first major league at-bat September 14.

1994   Injures knee in spring training and misses entire season.

1995   Atlanta Braves win first World Series since moving from
Milwaukee in 1966.

1996   Signs four-year contract with Atlanta for $8.25 million.

1998   Braves play in seventh consecutive NLCS.

1999   Awarded National League Most Valuable Player Award.

STATISTICS

ATLANTA BRAVES

Year	Team	G	AB	R	H	2B	3B	HR	RBI	BB	AVG.
1993	Atl N	8	3	2	2	1	0	0	0	1	.667
1994	Injured										
1995		140	524	87	139	22	3	23	86	73	.265
1996		157	598	114	185	32	5	30	110	87	.309
1997		157	597	100	176	41	3	21	111	76	.295
1998		160	601	123	188	29	5	34	107	96	.313
1999		157	567	116	181	41	1	45	110	126	.314
2000		156	579	118	180	38	1	36	111	95	.311
Totals		**935**	**3469**	**660**	**1051**	**204**	**18**	**189**	**635**	**554**	**.303**

World Series											
1995		6	21	3	6	3	0	0	1	4	.286
1996		6	21	3	6	3	0	0	3	4	.286
Totals		**12**	**42**	**6**	**12**	**6**	**0**	**0**	**4**	**8**	**.286**

FURTHER READING

Goodman, Michael. *Atlanta Braves*. Mankato, MN: Creative Education, 1998.

Kramer, Sydelle A. *Baseball's Greatest Hitters*. New York: Random Books for Young Readers, 1995.

Rosenberg, I. J. *Simply the Best! The Inside Story of the 1996 Atlanta Braves*. Marietta, GA: Longstreet Press Inc., 1996.

Schnert, Chris W. *Atlanta Braves*. Minneapolis, MN: Abdo & Daughters, 1997.

Stewart, Mark. *Baseball: The History of the National Pastime*. New York: Franklin Watts, 1998.

Index

Picture Credits
AP/Wide World Photos: pp. 2, 8, 11, 12, 29, 32, 35, 36, 40, 43, 46, 48, 50, 52,
54, 58; Courtesy of the Richmond Braves: pp. 22, 24, 26; University Microfilms,
Inc.: pp. 14, 18

BILL ZACK has spent 20 years as a sportswriter and has been the Atlanta Braves beat writer for the *Gwinnett Daily News* and *Morris Communications* since 1987. He has won numerous national and state writing awards, including the prestigious Green Eyeshade Award for sports reporting, and is the author of TOMAHAWKED!, an inside look at the Braves detailing the 1992 season. He is also a regular contributor to *The Sporting News* and has served as president of the Atlanta chapter of the Baseball Writers Association of America.

JIM MURRAY, who passed away in 1998, was a veteran sports columnist of the *Los Angeles Times*, and one of America's most acclaimed writers. He was named "America's Best Sportswriter" by the National Association of Sportscasters and Sportswriters 14 times, was awarded the Red Smith Award, and was twice winner of the National Headliner Award. In addition, he was awarded the J. G. Taylor Spink Award in 1987 for "meritorious contributions to baseball writing." With this award came his 1988 induction into the National Baseball Hall of Fame in Cooperstown, New York. In 1990, Jim Murray was awarded the Pulitzer Prize for Commentary.

EARL WEAVER is the winningest manager in the Baltimore Orioles' history by a wide margin. He compiled 1,480 victories in his 17 years at the helm. After managing eight different minor league teams, he was given the chance to lead the Orioles in 1968. Under his leadership the Orioles finished lower than second place in the American League East only four times in 17 years. One of only 12 managers in big league history to have managed in four or more World Series, Earl was named Manager of the Year in 1979. The popular Weaver had his number, 5, retired in 1982, joining Brooks Robinson, Frank Robinson, and Jim Palmer, whose numbers were retired previously. Earl Weaver continues his association with the professional baseball scene by writing, broadcasting, and coaching.